A Book of Testimonies

By

Kids Today Scholars Tomorrow™

KIDS TODAY - SCHOLARS TOMORROW™
OF THE
WORLD'S CHURCH OF THE LIVING GOD
CHATTANOOGA, TN

Acknowledgements

The testimonies in this book were written by the young people who participate in Kids Today Scholars Tomorrow. Kids Today Scholars Tomorrow is an organization created by Bishop W.C. Hunter with the primary purpose of reinforcing the wisdom taught in our ministry and in the educational system. During one of our meetings, it was suggested by a student that they would like to compose a testimony book to explain how the ministry has changed their lives. As a result of that recommendation, a testimony book was developed. As you read, the writing will describe their challenges, their vision for the future, finding their passions, and will explain how the word of God and our church family has influenced them.

Special thanks and much appreciation is extended to Pastor Allan Harrington and the late Bishop W.C. Hunter. We are grateful for the profound impact each of these men of God has had on our lives and the lives of our children. Their encouragement, spiritual guidance, love for the flock of God, and motivation have enhanced the lives of many. Special thanks to our committee members for Kids Today Scholars Tomorrow for their time and commitment to the students. We express our sincere gratitude to Brandis Smith and Jordan Pauldin who helped bring this book to life with their visual art and advice. Thank You.

The World's Church
OF THE LIVING GOD

Bishop W.C. Hunter

Bishop W.C. Hunter was the former pastor, teacher, and overseer of The World's Church of the Living God for 52 years. He departed this life December 11, 2016.

Pastor Allan Harrington

Pastor Allan Harrington is the anointed and appointed pastor, shepherd, and overseer of The World's Church of the Living God, Chattanooga, TN.

Contents

"I am Alpha and Omega, the beginning and the end, the first and the last." Revelation 22:13

This scripture resonates with me because God is everything, and it all begins and ends with Him. It reminds me that I should be full of praise and thanksgiving every day for all that He has created me to be and the life that He allows me to live.

-Sydney

Sydney
Grade 10

I Can Thank God for So Much

I thank God every day for waking me up and letting me see another beautiful day of life. It is around this time of Thanksgiving that I realize even more all the blessings and gifts He has given me. God has blessed me with amazing parents, a great sister, and a wonderful family. He has also blessed me to overcome situations in my life, most of which are typical teenage things; but lessons I needed to learn nonetheless. Great or small, the Father has guided me every step of the way through every circumstance. This life God has given me has been a favored one and I could not be more grateful.

We have been taught by Bishop Hunter and Pastor Allan Harrington to value education. My parents also encourage my sister and I to always aspire to do our best in school. To do just enough is not acceptable but to go above and beyond is how we succeed. This is where I thrive and excel. I love learning and the things I have accomplished in school so far, I owe all glory to God. I am an 'A' student, an Honor Society member, and I participate in various student clubs. Some concepts come easy for me (like math) and others are a challenge, but when I do well, it is rewarding. Despite whatever talents or abilities I possess, I recognize that God is the reason for my success.

Throughout my life the Lord has truly kept His hands upon me. He has seen me through several physical challenges. Even as a little girl I suffered from recurring stomach pain. I would have to take certain medicines and miss lots of days in school. But the man of God prayed for me, and today, by God's grace, those stomach aches are a thing of the past. More recently, I suffered a back injury while playing soccer. It affected my daily life and limited my activities in so many ways. My parents prayed for me, but they also reminded me that God is my Father too, and I can pray to Him for myself. With time, God healed me. "With His stripes we are healed", and I was.

Sometimes growing up can be tough. There are many lessons to learn. Through the word of God, I have also learned that our life should be about service. I have discovered that I enjoy helping people, particularly in academics. Many times, my peers have come to me for help. I always want them to do their best like I try to do. If I can help them accomplish their goals, then I also feel I've served a purpose. And I liked feeling needed and being useful in that way. Unexpectedly though, in this experience it turned out there was another lesson for me to learn. I am sure that I will carry it with me for the rest of my life. I had to use wisdom on how I choose to help someone. I had to learn to see people for who they are, especially ones that called themselves my friend. Sometimes there are boundaries that should not be crossed, and sometimes what you intend for good can be taken the wrong way. God had to open my eyes to these things and give me understanding.

There is nothing He can't do! And with Him, anything is possible. Without Him nothing is possible. My Lord and Savior has provided me with so much that I am eternally thankful . I could ask for nothing more than to have the Lord in my life.

"Remember now thy Creator in the days of thy youth, while the evil days come not, nor the years draw nigh, when though shalt say, I have no pleasure in them;" Ecclesiastes 12:1

This is my favorite scripture because it constantly reminds me to put God first in everything I do. It also puts things into perspective because I realize that I am not going to be young forever; therefore, I need to do everything I can to live a life according to how God wants me to before it is too late. God has blessed me every step of my life so far, and I know He will be with me every step of the way throughout the rest of my days.

-John

John
Grade 12

Before you read the rest of this essay, I need you to take a second to think about some of the things God has done for you in your life. Where were you when He first found you? What condition were you in? How far has He brought you since? Where would you be if it were not for God in your life? We as children of God should have an answer for all of those questions because we have been blessed with so much. We all have our own story that separates us from each other; however, we all end up with the same result— eternal life and salvation with Jesus. Throughout my short story of life, God has done a few things that have changed my life such as: saved my soul, blessed me to grow up in The World's Church of the Living God, WCLG, and blessed me to overcome a nagging knee injury.

The most marvelous thing God has done for me in my life is to save my soul from eternal torment. I will forever be grateful for His choosing because He did not have to choose me: my spot could have easily been someone else's, but God saw fit to choose me. I will always be indebted to the Father because there is no price that could equal having eternal life. Being a chosen one of God makes me feel special. It is like the feeling you get when you heard your parents say, "We are proud of you!" as a little kid, but on a much larger scale. Wouldn't we all love to hear those words: "Well done, my good and faithful servant." coming from our Heavenly Father? Longing to hear those words just conforms you to do right; well, it should! Being a child of God has been the best thing that has ever happened to me. I feel sorry for those who are not saved, especially because I know what their end result is; however, I am even more grateful because I know what my end result will be. I wouldn't trade it for anything or anyone. Salvation is something that is not earned; it is a gift that was given specifically to you. Knowing that God chose to give the gift of salvation to me makes me want to do His will even more because it's the least we can do. This is how my life has been changed by God saving my soul.

Another thing God has done for me that has changed my life is placed me inside of WCLG (The World's Church of the Living God). The World's Church of the Living God will forever have a special place in my heart. It has had the biggest impact on my life outside of my home. From a young age, I have been willing and ready to always go to church. I am glad that going to church has not become just a Sunday routine to me because there is always something to be heard that can aid me in my life. Hearing the Word from Bishop Hunter and Pastor Al has laid a solid foundation for my life. I can't mention The World's Church of the Living God without mentioning the saints. The saints have shown me so much support. I feel like I have been raised by a village: from giving advice, words of encouragement, tutoring, and athletic training. The church has been there for me through everything. This is how God has changed my life by placing me in The World's Church of the Living God.

We have all been plagued by a physical issue before, whether it be sickness, body aches, or any other thing that might come up. In August of 2018, I fully dislocated my knee. I had some of the craziest thoughts such as: I can't play basketball again, will I be able to walk, and I don't want people feeling sorry for me. I was a big baby throughout the whole recovery process. The doctor told me that the recovery process was six months; however, God blessed, and I made a full recovery in two months. This event changed my life because it helped me realize the things that were most important to me. I developed a sense of gratitude whenever I was able to do all of my normal activities again because I realized that everything I have could be taken away from me any second. At that point is where I think a lot of my maturity took place because it was mostly mental. I was always reminded that a merry heart does good like a medicine; therefore, causing me to stop feeling sorry for myself. I thank God for the injury I had because it brought me closer to Him. I still can't thank the saints enough for all the prayers and encouragement that they gave me throughout the process. This is how God used an injury to change my life in a positive way.

In conclusion, God has done a lot of things that have changed my life such as: saving my soul, placing me in The World's Church of the Living God and blessing me to overcome a knee injury. We never know how God will use different challenges to bring us closer to Him. That is why we must put all of our trust in Him and not lean on our own understanding. Don't take any of your blessings for granted because you could easily be on the opposite end of the spectrum. Now that I have come to the end of my essay, I would like for you to think again about the great things God has done for you. Think about the little things, think about the major things, and think about the feeling you had when you overcame. Never go a day without being thankful to God! I hope and pray that you enjoyed reading a little bit about how God has blessed me.

"Hast thou not known? Hast thou not heard, that the everlasting God, the Lord, the Creator of the ends of the earth, fainteth not, neither is weary? There is no searching of His understanding. He giveth power to the faint, and to them that have no might He increaseth strength. Even the youths shall faint and be weary, and the young men shall utterly fall. But they that wait upon the Lord shall renew their strength; they shall mount up with the wings as eagles; they shall run, and not be weary; and they shall walk, and not faint."
Isaiah 40: 28-31

These scriptures assure me that, as a human, I will fall short sometimes, but with God there is nothing impossible for me. I will be able to walk and not faint because He gives me the strength I lack. He created all things, and He is the King of Kings: with Him I can do anything.

-Aniyah

Aniyah
Grade 11

Clarity, passion, and honesty—God has revealed these three things to me in totally different ways, and I am extremely grateful. When I was younger, I never felt like I would ever find what I wanted out of my life. Sports were not my thing, the arts were uninteresting, and anything else I was exposed to, at that time was not for me. I just knew that I wanted to please God. I prayed for Him to lead me and guide me in the right direction to please Him and to be happy. Now, as a young woman, God has truly allowed me to see things in a completely different light. I have been shown the importance of honesty, led to find my passion, and given the gift of clarity. For these things, I will forever be grateful.

In middle school I was searching for something that I felt like I was amazing in, and I came up short every time. I was already comfortable with those activities, and they did not push me in any way. An opportunity came up that allowed me to come up with a product and sell it at a marketplace. I was truly terrified to do this. I thought I would not be able to come up with a product good enough to be bought by actual customers. I felt like God brought my friend, Avery, in my life to push me out of my comfort zone because without her I would still be searching for my passion. We came up with the name Natural Beauty. We made and sold the Natural Beauty products and won first place at the marketplace. We had the most votes and made almost one thousand dollars. Even though the business did not prevail, I made my own brand and found one of my passions. My business has taught me so much about myself, others, and the world around me. But God has been with me through this whole journey that has forever changed my life.

Honesty is something that people always hold to a high standard. I have always been taught to just tell the truth. Bishop Hunter and Pastor Al always teach on the importance of honesty and why you should always be honest. As I got older, I truly started to see myself and how important it was and its effect on the situation that I encounter every day. Seeing how people respond to honesty is one way that I saw its importance. And seeing people lie to cover themselves never turned out good. This showed me that honesty, no matter how bad it may be, is the best thing to do. When you are honest, things can be fixed, but when you lie, nothing can be resolved. Lastly, God showed me how lying not only affects the liar, but it also affects the receiver of the lies. Lies ultimately hurt people, no matter how small. The lies grow and spiral out of control and can leave a long-lasting effect. I have come to realize that if I lie, it not only affects me but my relationship with God, and it changes my relationship with others.

Clarity – *the quality of transparency or purity, the quality of being coherent and intelligible.* Being able to see things clearly and illuminated by the light of God makes situations much easier to handle or to recover. God really has brought me understanding and comfort. I feel that this pandemic has brought me closer to God and His word. God has truly shown me what He can do and to not worry amidst tough times. He has opened my eyes to my potential and the great things that I can do. My business and my schooling have changed due to the things that God has shown me during these times, and I am extremely grateful and pray that God will continue to provide me understanding, clarity, and wisdom as I continue my life. These words have gained a new meaning to me as I have gotten older. God has really shown me favor in my life, and all these things are not even the tip of the iceberg of the things He has done for me. These are just the things that I can fully explain and clearly understand. I love God and pray He continues to cover me and lead my life.

"...faith without works is dead"
James 2:20

This is one of my favorite scriptures because I believe it is important to apply the scriptures in your everyday life.

-Ajay

Ajay
Grade 12

As I look back over my past years, I can tell that I am truly blessed. I have been blessed to grow mentally and physically in our ministry. Through the teaching of Bishop W.C. Hunter and Pastor Allan Harrington, I have learned the importance of what participation and dedication in the ministry means. Being able to be a part of this ministry was the best thing that could have ever happened for me because not only did it introduce the TRUE GOD but also a true loving family.

As a child, I was raised in the church with my grandparents due to the passing of my mother. Being the youngest of three brothers, I was not able to spend much time with my mother before she passed. But with God's provision, He placed love in my grandparents' hearts to take us. My two brothers struggled to adjust to the changes. This took a big toll on our family. However, with the love and support of the ministry, God took care of us and sculpted us into the family we have become today. God has taken care of us and made sure, even without a biological mother, we have the strength to keep moving forward.

Being raised in the ministry has done the most for me. I was exposed to the truth and introduced to who God; my true Father is. From this, through the years I have learned how to grow my relationship with Him. As a babe in the ministry, I was always fascinated with the program held at the beginning of each service. This represented the welcoming of the Lord of Host, God, into the building and giving total praise to Him. Influenced by my older brother, I joined the New Youth Breed of America led by Coach William Ballard Sr. This program was not just for show. It was a testimony, showing how God, through it all, fights for us in this wicked world. With all the members believing this, we showed unity. Just by doing this, I could tell that God was there, and He is with us. The Spirit of the Lord has been with this group on many occasions, regardless of the number of members.

God has blessed me over the years to strengthen my comprehension of knowledge. Going to church every Sunday as a child, I always knew that we were there for a good reason, but I did not really understand the principles and knowledge that was given. With the help of my grandparents coaching me on how to focus in church, I began to comprehend what was being said. I began to realize that it was way more to it than just getting up going to church every Sunday. It was and is still today more of receiving the revelation out of the message and applying that to your everyday life...from obey your parents in the sight of the Lord for this is right, to I can do all things in Christ who strengthens me. These are just a few major keys needed to please God and to live longer on earth.

Being able to say that I am a child of God is an honorable thing. It is more than just the notion of going to church, of knowing God's ways, and of knowing that we are in a **royal priesthood**. We realize that the things we do are only for God and to serve His people. Knowing this and putting it into practice, I have learned over the course of the years that you differentiate yourself from the world and its doing. I am so thankful that I was born into this ministry. Had it not been for God, I would not be the growing man I am today.

"...I will never leave thee, nor forsake thee" Hebrews 13:5

I tend to feel like I'm alone, and this scripture helps me to remember that God will never leave me.

–Madison

Madison
Grade 7

Being a Christian is just a statement. There are millions of Christians out there in the world but very few believers. I am sure that most believers have a testimony that is very candid in their lives. Although God has changed my life, just for being my Father, there are three specifics that come to mind: He saved my soul, He helped make me a better person, and He helped me pursue my talents. One thing God has done that has changed my life was that He saved my soul. Being saved isn't about being baptized or being the first one on the church pew. It's about believing that Jesus Christ died for your sins. I was saved when I was six years old. At that moment, I realized that I had believed that Jesus was our Lord and Savior and that I was ready for His spirit to be entered into me. It wasn't until this year that I felt like I was developing a real relationship with Him. Being saved doesn't just mean you have a green card into heaven. It is about really accepting God and allowing Him to guide you through life.

Another thing God has done that has changed my life was that He helped me get to a better place as a person. Two years ago, I suffered from some mental health issues. I was being bullied at school, and I didn't practice healthy coping mechanisms. I hid it and buried it deep and it wasn't until I prayed and talked to the Father that I realized I needed to do something about it. I talked to my mom, and she helped me a lot. I realized that I am not always going to feel 100%, and that is okay. Whenever I asked God about what to do it was crystal clear. Realizing that I need to work on myself with the help of God was the best decision I have ever made.

Lastly but not least, God has changed my life by allowing me to see I have talents. I have read the scripture about the talents multiple times, but it wasn't until recently that I realized what it meant and how it applied to me and my life. I like to dance, act, sing, write, and draw sometimes. I never realized how fortunate I was that God has allowed me to use my talents. Once I realized what the scripture meant, I became really aware of how to use them: I go to dance three times a week, I am writing a book just for fun, I sing all the time, I draw for school, and I am very dramatic! I am very grateful for all my talents, and I will forever be using them all throughout my life.

Having been born into The World's Church of the Living God, nothing about the message has changed, but the way I have received it has definitely changed. God has changed my life particularly by saving my soul, by guiding me into the right direction, and by helping me amplify my talents.

"Fear thou not; for I am with thee; be not dismayed; for I am thy God: I will strengthen thee; yea, I will help thee; yea, I will uphold thee with the right hand of My righteousness."
Isaiah 41:10

I chose this verse because it helps me get through times when I want to give up on things, and when I am going through stressful times.

-Addison

Addison
Grade 7

The Things God Has Done That Changed My Life

Three things that God has done to help change my life are my salvation when God saved me, overcoming what one of my teachers said I could not do, and believing in the truth. These are the main things for which I am thankful that He changed in my life. He has helped me overcome, and there is still more to come, I know.

The first thing that God changed in my life was my salvation. He opened my eyes to what I was missing in life. After I got saved, my mind started to understand things better. I am thankful that I got saved because it has helped me with some of the most challenging things that the devil has tried to throw at me. God has helped direct and lead me in the path that He wants for me.

The second thing that God has changed in my life was what my third-grade teacher had said -- that I would not be able to read and understand anything. When she said that, I prayed about it and started working harder. My hard work paid off because it got me to where I am now. God has helped me prove her wrong, even though she still doubted me. I overcame it and made star roll! The way she had said that to me was the devil trying to tear me down and not let me succeed. I thank God for letting me get past that grade and to understand things that she said I would never understand.

The third thing is that God has helped me believe in the truth. Although we study the Bible at school, I know what the real truth is no matter what my teacher says. By knowing the truth, I can spread God's word to people around me. Also, when I have to learn a new Bible verse, I already know what it actually means. God has truly helped me understand what I learned for school by knowing the truth.

In conclusion, God has changed my life through salvation, overcoming my teacher's doubts, and knowing the right way things are supposed to be. These have been challenging moments for me but, with the help of God, I have been able to improve, to progress, and to be successful. I thank the Lord for all He has helped me overcome, and I expect even more opportunities. I hope this has inspired you to not give up, and to believe in God no matter what is going on around you.

"And we know that all things work together for good to them that love God, to them who are the called according to His purpose."
Romans 8:28

This scripture is one of my favorites because I know I love God. I know that no matter what challenges I face in life with God all things are possible, and you can do anything through Jesus Christ.

-Meghan

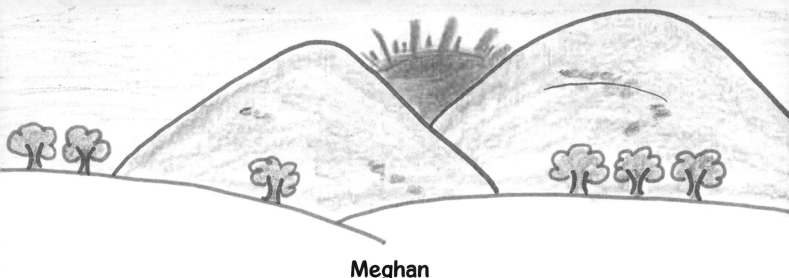

Meghan
Grade 8

On April 18, 2007, I was welcomed into this world by two proud parents. My mother has told me numerous times how I literally slept the entire first month of my life. I may have been in and out of sleep, but I imagine hearing the voices all around me. Some voices were soothing, comforting, and very familiar, and every once in a while, some new voices. I grew a little older; then I heard the voice of Bishop W.C. Hunter who taught me the word of God and introduced me to JESUS. On August 26, 2018, my ears heard the sweetest, most important voice of all calling to me, and I answered. I gave my life to JESUS. I am so thankful each and every day of my life. I am only a teenager now, but even in these few years, I have learned so much. God has blessed my life in many ways through my faith, family, education, and healings.

The word of God has made me realize that I can do anything if I believe, have faith, and trust in God. It has helped me with challenges in my life, and some I am still figuring it out as a young teen. I have also learned how important it is to be thankful and grateful for what you have and don't take it for granted. I am truly thankful that God blessed me to grow up in this ministry where the truth is taught. I have learned how to live life through God.

I am thankful that God blessed me with my family and parents. The word of God has made me realize that everything I have done or accomplished was in God's favor. He has blessed me with a wonderful education, including my recent induction into the NJHS (National Junior Honor Society). He has also allowed me to be a part of the Advanced/Gifted program and to continue to be a Star/Honor roll student.

God has blessed me so many times in helping me overcome problems and injuries. He blessed me to not have any complications after I dislocated my left knee. He also helped me overcome a breathing problem that I used to deal with as a young child.

Therefore, with God all things are possible. There is nothing He cannot do. God has blessed me in so many ways that I cannot even possibly explain. These are just some of the many ways God has blessed me in my life!

"Who shall separate us from the love of Christ? Shall tribulation, or distress, or persecution, or famine, or nakedness, or peril, or sword?...Nay in all these things we are more than conquerors through Him that loved us."
Romans 8:35-37

This is my favorite scripture because it brings me comfort knowing that absolutely nothing can separate me from God.

-Makenzie

Makenzie
Grade 10

A Glass Half-full

Encouraging words push people to keep fighting to realize what they have, and never give up on it. I thank God for my ministry, and for the stable community I am always welcome to associate in. God has blessed the saints to love me through whatever or wherever life takes me. Our ministry serves as a place where everyone is in one accord; we are a beautiful family of born-again believers.

Reflecting over my high school career I know that it has been limited, but I am thankful for it. I hope that my world will expand and the opportunities are endless. Early on, I realized how extensively God has blessed my household; as I have gotten older, He has continued to use the ministry to uplift me. However, I did not want to take any success for granted. So, I started working. God blessed me to pick up what I could handle, and from the beginning I could see how it helped. Our birthday parties got bigger; we adopted a dog, and I was even blessed with my own she-shed. Sometimes a sacrifice is worth more in the long run than it is in the exact moment. God has allowed me to see and act with a selfless attitude from then on. Even though I might have missed a few events or excitement that comes with high school, God blessed me to never stay bitter. He blessed that I would remain thankful for what I had rather than focusing on what I could not obtain, even if He used saints to do it. My glass has remained optimistically half-full, looking for and appreciating God's grace even through the harder times.

Over the past few years, I have observed myself forming into the woman I hope to become one day. It is hard to say now, who I will be in just a few years, but I can say that I have learned to walk in who I truly am. I have learned to identify with what God has made me to be. The intimate and close-knit KTST group has served as a sounding board through my teenage years. They are apart of my village, as I am apart of theirs. KTST has encouraged me to be a selfless, independent woman. Helping to sustain a group built around loving others and giving back to your community has humbled me, and I plan to continue as an alumni even through adulthood. I have a purpose in my ministry. I can give back to the people who conjointly helped me become the strong woman I will be. I thank God for the opportunity to serve His people.

My grandmother once told me, "It takes a village to raise a child". My friend reminded me, "You can do all things through Christ..." A church sister once sent me her notes from a Sunday message I missed. I thank God for the ministry and how much they have contributed to me, mentally and physically. They believe in me and hold me up to a reasonable standard for success. As I stated before, encouraging words push people to keep fighting, and somehow the right words find their way to us when we need them the most. It has always been my Ma and me, along with immediate family. However, there is comfort in knowing there is a strong body of individuals willing to go above and beyond for my well-being. So, the church is my village, that my grandmother expressed. I can do all things through Christ, as I am reminded daily. Along with, I know my sisters and brothers in the church have my back. God blessed me with a fulfilling lifestyle and unconditional loving ministry. Thank you, God, for putting these people and group in place to welcome me in, for putting it on their hearts to care for me. I pray that I can continue to be active in the ministry that changes lives, and the Scholarship group that believes in opportunity. I pray my view on life will forever remain at least half-full.

"Make a joyful noise unto the Lord, all ye lands. Serve the Lord with gladness: come before His presence with singing." Psalms 100: 1-2

This scripture is my favorite because it reminds me that God is with me no matter how far I go.

–Santana

Santana
Grade 11

God has blessed me throughout my life. He has given me a loving ministry, family, and friends. I could not have asked for a better environment to grow up in. I find comfort, in the fact, that I know no matter where I go; God is always watching out for me. I know that He has a plan for me even if I can't see it yet. As I grow older, I begin to understand more of what the word says, and how I should apply it to my everyday life; I was given the gift of clarity. For these things, I will forever be grateful.

I thank God for my mom and dad because of the sacrifices they make for me even when they don't have to. Sending me to Girls Preparatory School is a great example of one of those sacrifices. I know that by being at that school; I am preparing myself for opportunities that others may not get to have, and for that I am extremely thankful. I am blessed to have parents who help guide me on the right path of success no matter what my career choice is. I see the unconditional love that God gives to us reflected in them.

The ministry has instilled in me the power of faith and community. Whether it is going to school and facing a big test or a major life decision; the church has taught me that faith is always the best answer. Faith is the foundation in all aspects for without it we would have nothing. The church has fostered every single one of my hobbies and talents, and to have a community that cares about you and genuinely wants to help you is to be admired. I hope by learning what I have in church, I can take this with me on any future endeavors, and that I won't forget that feeling of community and faith.

I thank God for the true friends I have had along the way that have grown with me. The word has taught me to distinguish those who will grow and stick with you for the better, and those who will act as your friend, but then do something spiteful against you. I am blessed to have found people who have positive energy and want to be in your life. I believe that once you surround yourself with those who want to be better, you become better. I was taught that the energy you surround yourself with matters. I thank Him for placing wonderful friends in my life; so that we thrive together.

In conclusion, God has placed so many blessings in my life that I am grateful for. My ministry, my family, friends, and school are a few of the many blessings I have received. The church has given me knowledge which I am now able to understand and apply in my life; so that it may guide me in things that I do. I pray I continue to find the many blessings He has given me and that others can do the same. Faith, community, love, and gratefulness are the traits I have seen in my different environments, and I am hopeful these traits follow me wherever God's plan takes me next.

"I can do all things through Christ which strengtheneth me."
Philippians 4:13

It is a powerful verse, and it provides comfort to me knowing that Christ is my strength and through Him I can do anything.

-Chloie

Chloie
Grade 10

I would like to start this testimony by saying that I am here by the grace of God. My mother always likes to tell others the story of how she found out she was pregnant. She had been suffering from a small cold and went to her doctor. The doctor told her that she would be suffering from the small cold for a few more months. My mom was very surprised because she had been told that she could not have children. Here her doctor was telling her that she was pregnant!!! I am here because I have a purpose. It was no mistake that a woman who could not have a child had one.

The Lord has always provided for me whether that was by placing certain people in my life or presenting opportunities for me. I am so thankful and blessed to know that I have people inside and outside of the church who are always there for me. The church has been a second home for me since I was little, and I am so grateful to be able to have known Pastor Hunter. He was a mentor to so many people, and I will always remember the life lessons he taught me. It is such a blessing to know that I have the word of God to guide my steps, and I can look to God's word when I am in need. To know that I have been presented with knowledge like this truly amazes me.

I will always be grateful for the church and the people inside of the church who always push me to be better and constantly show love and support. This is my testimony – a testimony of purpose and gratitude.

"O Lord, thou hast searched me, and known me.
Thou knowest my downsitting and mine uprising,
thou understandest my thought afar off."
Psalm 139:1-2

"Fear thou not; for I am with thee: be
not dismayed for I am thy God..."
Isaiah 41:10

The reason I chose them both is because to me
they go together. Psalm 139 talks about how God
created us. He knew me before anybody else:
before I was even thought of. No matter where
we go or no matter what we are going through,
God is always standing right beside us. In Isaiah
41, He specifically says that I will never leave you.
He reassures me that even through the hardest
things my God can make a way.

–Chelsea

Chelsea
Grade 12

Passion is defined as a strong feeling or emotion one feels. This drives you; it wakes you up every morning and helps you rest every night. It burns in your heart and tells your story, sometimes without you saying a word. I am going to tell you about the time God gave me a gift which is my passion.

At the start of first grade, I transferred to a new school. Being the new kid on the block, I did not have many friends. I often felt excluded during games, projects, and even by my teachers. I never truly understood what people did not like about me. I tried my best to be kind to everyone with whom my paths crossed, but regardless of what I did, no one would accept me. After a few years passed, nothing seemed to change. I made a few acquaintances, but I still felt left out. During this time, I was diagnosed with attention deficit hyperactivity disorder. My teachers were unsure how to assist me when I got distracted. So, this led to me being isolated from the rest of the class. I was put in a corner of the classroom where I was told to sit quietly and do my work. Rather than focusing on my work, I spent my time wondering why I was being punished for something I could not control.

Because of my lack of friends and the isolation I felt from the teachers, I knew I needed another way to express myself. My father encouraged me to begin auditioning for many different things, including singing and acting. He knew performing would be a good way to make friends and learn more about myself. So, I auditioned for the school's choir in the third grade. I had always enjoyed singing and acting, and one day God showed me it was my passion. I was trying out for the song, "I will Always Love You", by Whitney Houston. I wanted the solo. Unfortunately, I did not know the song very well. My music teacher, Shier Thrower, gave us the weekend to learn it. I came back and got the chance to try again. My teacher looked at me and said, "The song is good, but you need to take that note, get mad, and throw it to the back of the wall." I did exactly what she told me to do, and I have been singing ever since then. The choir gave me hope and many opportunities to sing many solos and make a few videos.

God revealed my gift to me, and I ran with it!! Now, I sing everywhere I go. Singing is my passion, and with that, I praise the Most High as a way of giving Him thanks for saving me and showing me a light out of darkness. By singing, I share my voice; hopefully, through me you see HIM.

"But the fruit of the Spirit is love, joy, peace, longsuffering, gentleness, goodness, faith, meekness, temperance..." Galatians 5:22

This is one of my favorite scriptures because it describes God's Spirit as something so gentle. When I am going into my day, I feel these characteristics of God's spirit within me.

-Naomi

Naomi
Grade 8

There have been many times where God has blessed me and allowed me to see the light even in my darkest moments. I am very thankful for everything that has been placed in my life: my friends, family, pets, including the way God has touch my life through music. When I was eleven years old, I started playing the clarinet which I found myself enjoying. My love for music through the grace of God brought me closer to my family. At the age of eight, I got my first dog; God revealed my passion for animals during these moments. God has touched my life through music, family and animals.

First, my life has been touched by God through music starting in my 7 th grade year in middle school. I was selected to be in the band class in school; I was not too happy about it at first. I eventually had to buy a clarinet for the class and get a beginner's book. As the quarter moved forward, we started playing music outside of the beginner's book that had more feeling and rhythm. My eyes were opened to the light of music pushing me to continue participating in band class. I became a really great player and was asked to join the marching band. I was more than happy to join. I grew to love the marching band so much that I knew this was something I wanted to do in college. This opened more college opportunities for me and is something I still love doing. God placed music in my life and opened a new door for my future for which I am grateful.

Secondly, God has touched my life through my immediate family. My family has been here for me since day one and has supported me in everything that I have decided to do. I could not ask for a family more caring, loving, and genuine. God allowed me to connect with my dad through the love of music. I have an amazing family who is still healthy, alive, and well. I am very thankful for my family.

Lastly, I have been motivated through my pets. God has allowed me to see how much I love animals. When I was only eight years old, I finally received the dog I really wanted. After having a dog for a while, I realized that it was something about animals that really inspired me to want to become a veterinarian. God placed a caring heart within me to want to protect animals in any way that I can. His goal is for me to care for animals and nurse them back to health. He stored the potential in me that I did not know I had. I am incredibly grateful for that.

In conclusion, God has blessed me in every aspect of my life, especially my music, my family, and animals. Despite not loving music initially, I love it now. I could not even pick my own family, but I am completely grateful and blessed with the family God gave me. Finally, my furry friends...or as I can say my pets...have always kept me in good spirits, and I only have God to thank for that. He instilled in me a passion for animals. God has blessed me and has shown me so much love even before I was brought on the face of the Earth, and I am thankful!

Fun, Relationships, Community

Mother/Son—Father/Daughter Dance
The Walden Club

Kids Today Scholars Tomorrow
Civil and Human Rights Museum

I AM...
CONFIDENT
I CAN...
ACHIEVE
I WILL...
SURPASS
WE WILL..
SUCCEED!!

About the Author

Kids Today Scholars Tomorrow is an organization created by Bishop W.C. Hunter with the goal of reinforcing the wisdom taught in their ministry and in the educational system.

Archway Publishing books may be ordered through booksellers or by contacting:

Archway Publishing
1663 Liberty Drive
Bloomington, IN 47403
www.archwaypublishing.com
844-669-3957

Interior Image Credit: Each Student

Scripture taken from the King James Version of the Bible.

ISBN: 978-1-6657-2300-8 (sc)
ISBN: 978-1-6657-2299-5 (e)

Library of Congress Control Number: 2022908241

Print information available on the last page.

Archway Publishing rev. date: 6/14/2022

Printed in the United States
by Baker & Taylor Publisher Services